CW00493388

# Greater Than a Tourist
# Book Series
# Reviews from Readers

I think the series is wonderful and beneficial for tourists to get information before visiting the city.

-Seckin Zumbul, Izmir Turkey

I am a world traveler who has read many trip guides but this one really made a difference for me. I would call it a heartfelt creation of a local guide expert instead of just a guide.

-Susy, Isla Holbox, Mexico

New to the area like me, this is a must have!

 -Joe, Bloomington, USA

This is a good series that gets down to it when looking for things to do at your destination without having to read a novel for just a few ideas.

-Rachel, Monterey, USA

Good information to have to plan my trip to this destination.

-Pennie Farrell, Mexico


Great ideas for a port day.

-Mary Martin USA


Aptly titled, you won't just be a tourist after reading this book. You'll be greater than a tourist!

-Alan Warner, Grand Rapids, USA


Even though I only have three days to spend in San Miguel in an upcoming visit, I will use the author's suggestions to guide some of my time there. An easy read - with chapters named to guide me in directions I want to go.

 -Robert Catapano, USA


Great insights from a local perspective! Useful information and a very good value!

 -Sarah, USA


This series provides an in-depth experience through the eyes of a local. Reading these series will help you to travel the city in with confidence and it'll make your journey a unique one.

-Andrew Teoh, Ipoh, Malaysia

# GREATER THAN A TOURIST- VERONA VENETO REGION ITALY

*50 Travel Tips from a Local*

Sabrina Beggiato

The statements in this book are of the authors and may not be the views of CZYK Publishing or Greater Than a Tourist.

First Edition

Cover designed by: Ivana Stamenkovic

Cover Image: https://pixabay.com/photos/church-cathedral-buildings-river-6579136/

CZYK Publishing Since 2011.
CZYKPublishing.com
Greater Than a Tourist

Lock Haven, PA
All rights reserved.
**ISBN:** 9798797614944

# >TOURIST

## 50 TRAVEL TIPS FROM A LOCAL

# BOOK DESCRIPTION

With travel tips and culture in our guidebooks written by a local, it is never too late to visit Verona. Greater Than a Tourist - Verona, Veneto region, Italy by author Sabrina Beggiato offers the inside scoop on the city of Love. Most travel books tell you how to travel like a tourist. Although there is nothing wrong with that, as part of the 'Greater Than a Tourist' series, this book will give you candid travel tips from someone who has lived at your next travel destination. This guide book will not tell you exact addresses or store hours but instead gives you knowledge that you may not find in other smaller print travel books. Experience cultural, culinary delights, and attractions with the guidance of a Local. Slow down and get to know the people with this invaluable guide. By the time you finish this book, you will be eager and prepared to discover new activities at your next travel destination.

Inside this travel guide book you will find:

Visitor information from a Local
Tour ideas and inspiration
Valuable guidebook information

Greater Than a Tourist- A Travel Guidebook with 50 Travel Tips from a Local. Slow down, stay in one place, and get to know the people and culture.

# OUR STORY

Traveling is a passion of the Greater than a Tourist book series creator. Lisa studied abroad in college, and for their honeymoon Lisa and her husband toured Europe. During her travels to Malta, an older man tried to give her some advice based on his own experience living on the island since he was a young boy. She was not sure if she should talk to the stranger but was interested in his advice. When traveling to some places she was wary to talk to locals because she was afraid that they weren't being genuine. Through her travels, Lisa learned how much locals had to share with tourists. Lisa created the Greater Than a Tourist book series to help connect people with locals. A topic that locals are very passionate about sharing.

# TABLE OF CONTENTS

Book Description

Our Story

Table of Contents

Dedication

About the Author

How to Use This Book

From the Publisher

WELCOME TO > TOURIST

INTRODUCTION

1.  Do You Love Someone? Take Them To Verona

2. Benvenuto! (Ben Veh Noo Toh)

3.  Monetine For Your Espresso (Cash For Your Coffee!)

4.  Go Ahead About 150 Metres, Turn Right, Go About 300 Metres And You Have Arrived!

5.  Mamma Mia! *Gestures*

6.  "Veronesi Tutti Matti' (Veronesi Are All Mad)

7.  I Get Around (Round, Get Around-Round-Round, Ooh) (Wah-Wah-Ooh)

8.  Coming By Car

9.  Your Best Options: Bus And Bike

10. Your Caffeine Fix, The Italian Way

11. Sweet Breakfast - "Cappuccino And Brioche".

12. Lunchtime: I Can Sense The Pasta Approaching

13. Where To Have Lunch

14. Merendina (Snacks)

15. The Sacred Aperitivo

16. More About Aperitivo (And Where To Have It)

17. Dinner Time In Italy

18. What To Eat - Typical Verona Foods

19. Must Try: Risotto All'Amarone And Polenta

20. Bigoli: We Took Spaghetti And Made It Better

21. Risotto With Tastasal

22. Pandoro (Our Dessert With A Patent) And The Competition With Panettone

23. Have 'Fritole'

24. Try "Tagliere Di Affettati"

25. When To Visit Verona

26. "A Vacation Is A Sunburn At Premium Prices." - Hal Chadwicke

27. Can You Visit Verona In One Day?

28. A Very Short And Super Interesting History Of Verona (Just Enough To Show You Know)

29. Visit The Arena Of Verona (Finally!)

30. Touch Le Tette Di Giulietta - (Yes That Means Boobs)

31. Obviously, Go Shopping (In Via Mazzini)

32. Walk Around Piazza Delle Erbe (One Of The Most Beautiful Squares In Italy!)

33. Consider Going Up To Torre Dei Lamberti (Some Steps!)

34. Definitely Go Up To Castel San Pietro (Some More Steps!)

35. Go Find Out Why I Love Castelvecchio So Much

36. Less Known Places In Verona

37. The Arche Scaligere And The Movable Gate

38. Go Shopping In The Middle Of Roman Ruins (Literally!)

39. The Secret Well Of Lovers (No, Not Romeo And Juliet)

40. Challenge Someone To Spot The Creator Of Arch Of The Gavi (Or The Subway Arch). Admire The Original Roman Stones Underneath!

41. We Love Pandoro So Much That We Made A Statue Of It. Or Maybe Two.

42. Learn Some Phrases - Language Basics

43. We actually say Mamma mia

44. Una Pizza, Per Favore (Oona Pee-Sa Pehr Fa – Voh – Reh)

45. The True Way To Speak Italian: Hand Gestures (Yes, You'll Need A Guide)

46. "Cono Or Coppetta?" Best Gelateria In Verona

47. What Souvenirs To Bring Home? Buy Some Groceries (Your Best Option).

48. Join The Locals At The Weekly Market

49.  Extra Time? Day Visit To Lake Garda

50.  Goditi A Pieno La Tua Vacanza!

TOP REASONS TO BOOK THIS TRIP

TRIVIA

ANSWERS

Packing and Planning Tips

Travel Questions

Travel Bucket List

NOTES

# DEDICATION

This book is dedicated to my brother, who served as a reviewer for this book and prevented me from writing a highly specific chapter on the functioning of the bidet. To Marek, who has wandered around Verona with me so many times that is the last person who needs to read this book. And to the beauty of this wonderful Paese.

# ABOUT THE AUTHOR

Joining the party in August 1998, in Verona, Sabrina has been eating, travelling and writing for most of her time here. She loves mugs, hot teas and gazing at beautiful landscapes from mountaintops after struggling to get there.

After years of working as a copywriter, writing a book about Verona and all things Italian is finally the perfect way to express her gratitude for this wonderful country and all the beauty it has to offer.

# HOW TO USE THIS BOOK

The *Greater Than a Tourist* book series was written by someone who has lived in an area for over three months. The goal of this book is to help travelers either dream or experience different locations by providing opinions from a local. The author has made suggestions based on their own experiences. Please check before traveling to the area in case the suggested places are unavailable.

**Travel Advisories**: As a first step in planning any trip abroad, check the Travel Advisories for your intended destination.
https://travel.state.gov/content/travel/en/traveladvisories/traveladvisories.html

# FROM THE PUBLISHER

Traveling can be one of the most important parts of a person's life. The anticipation and memories that you have are some of the best. As a publisher of the Greater Than a Tourist, as well as the popular *50 Things to Know* book series, we strive to help you learn about new places, spark your imagination, and inspire you. Wherever you are and whatever you do I wish you safe, fun, and inspiring travel.

Lisa Rusczyk Ed. D.
CZYK Publishing

# WELCOME TO
## > TOURIST

*The Roman Ponte Pietra in Verona*

*The Lion of Saint Mark, located in Piazza delle Erbe, the symbol of the Venetian Republic*

*Verona Arena*

*The balcony of Juliet's house*

In west Verona born and raised...

Indeed, I was born in a small town in Verona and grew up there. Mum and dad have been changing my nappies and clothes around the city, at the lake, and in nearby Venetian towns since I was this tall. Now I dress up all by myself, but the passion for this precious part of Italy hasn't faded.

At secondary school I found out that I really enjoy writing. So, a scientific high school diploma and a degree in Languages for International Trade from Verona later, I began working as a content creator for various sites and companies.

I have studied and travelled in various parts of Europe, but my final destination has always been my home, in Verona.

At the time of writing, it's now time for me to leave my hometown once again. Even though I am about to move abroad to follow my writing dreams, leaving Verona is difficult. I know every corner of it and I have figured out all my favourite places: the best gelateria, the perfect coffee shop where to study and relax, the most heart-warming view from the Castle San Pietro and my favourite spot in the park of Castelvecchio.

13

Still, I embrace this change, knowing full well that even if I find a new favourite coffee shop, pizzeria and park, Verona will always remain my Verona, it is part of me and it translates into everything I create. I will never stop writing about it. And of course, I will go back as soon as I have the chance.

I want to share with you my insight and all the tips I have to make you get the most out of your stay. Maybe we'll see each other around, having a Spritz at the Osteria del Bugiardo or dancing around in the square of Castelvecchio, but for now, I'm glad I have the chance to make you fall in love with this beautiful city.

# INTRODUCTION

*"I may not have gone where I
intended to go, but I think I have
ended up where I needed to be."*

–Douglas Adams. 'The Long Dark Tea-Time of the
Soul.'

Verona, the city of love, Romeo and Juliet, of
good risotto, Pandoro, cheap delicious
Spritz, and many other treasures. A
UNESCO gem since 2000, it has to be visited at least
once in a lifetime with an ice-cream in one hand, a
camera in the other and many steps on your way.

In this book I'll give you my tips to visit Verona
from the perspective of someone who has lived there
most of her life and loves it immensely. I hope this
will make you enjoy your stay as much as I'm grateful
for this beautiful city.

## Verona
Province of Verona, Italy

# Verona
# Italy
# Climate

|  | High | Low |
|---|---|---|
| January | 44 | 30 |
| February | 48 | 32 |
| March | 57 | 39 |
| April | 64 | 45 |
| May | 74 | 54 |
| June | 81 | 61 |
| July | 86 | 65 |
| August | 85 | 65 |
| September | 77 | 57 |
| October | 65 | 48 |
| November | 53 | 39 |
| December | 44 | 31 |

## GreaterThanaTourist.com

Temperatures are in Fahrenheit degrees.
Source: NOAA

# 1. DO YOU LOVE SOMEONE? TAKE THEM TO VERONA

Verona is made of stone streets, antique squares, narrow streets and courtyards, colours, and small shops. It is made of students who get lost in the University and run from the Ateneo to the station. It is made of tourists with noses in the air, bags full of typical products, cameras in their hands and hats on their heads. It is made of locals who no longer know how to dodge all the others and fill the secondary streets.

Verona is made of heartbeats, because in the city of Romeo and Juliet's passion you can't help but fall in love.

I have lived in Verona for most of my life and, although I may seem a little biased, I can say one thing with confidence: Verona is beautiful. Full stop. It is one of Italy's greatest cities of artistic interest, an Italian gem that deserves to be visited, and has been a UNESCO World Heritage Site since 2000.

I have travelled to various European cities and lived abroad, but coming home to my home town Verona is always an unspeakable joy.

# 2. BENVENUTO! (BEN VEH NOO TOH)

Benvenuto in Italia! Before we delve into the delights that Verona, my city, has to offer, it is wiser to give you an introduction to the basics you need to know before stepping into the Bel Paese, my boot-with-a-heel shaped country.

These are the most practical and useful aspects. Once they are set, you'll get to enjoy your holiday to the fullest, without any worries. Maybe you will even be mistaken for an Italian.

Let's talk about which coins to use to get coffee, how best to find your way around and many other tricks. Hang in there with me and I will reveal to you the best gelateria in Verona, I promise!

# 3. MONETINE FOR YOUR ESPRESSO (CASH FOR YOUR COFFEE!)

We are in Italy! The currency is Euro (€). Here you can pay by card in the vast majority of places, and your bank will automatically convert your currency. Watch out for hidden fees.

If you have cash in your own currency unfortunately it will not be accepted. But you can exchange it at post offices or banks in the centre. Stay away from exchange offices, hotels and airports, as the commissions there are very high and you could lose up to a third of your money.

Important: although almost all shops in Italy accept credit cards, sometimes smaller businesses such as bars, grocery shops, craft or souvenir shops will only accept them for purchases over a certain amount (usually over €5).

This is especially true if you have coffee at a small neighbourhood bar and spend €1, €1.30: be prepared to be asked to pay with cash!

When in doubt, your best option is to pop your head into a shop and ask directly if you can pay with card.

I thought this was the norm, so when I was abroad and paid 0.50€ using my card, I was shocked. I stared at the shop assistant in amazement. She must have wondered what was wrong with me.

Are you about to go out for a cappuccino and brioche with friends? Or maybe a delicious spritz? Check that you have "monetine" in your wallet!

# 4. GO AHEAD ABOUT 150 METRES, TURN RIGHT, GO ABOUT 300 METRES AND YOU HAVE ARRIVED!

I gave these directions to a tourist once, and I saw panic in his eyes. I thought I had said some sort of bullshit, but he then explained that he had no idea how much a metre is!

In Italy, we use the metric system. A metre is approximately 3 feet, a little more than a yard, and 39 inches. Roughly, a refrigerator's width. Let me know if I've forgotten anything.

Jokes aside, to make things easier for you, a metre is approximately the length of one long step. An average step is about 74 cm (and 100 cm is one metre). I'm not saying you should count every step until you reach your destination, but at least now you have an idea.

# 5. MAMMA MIA! *GESTURES*

Don't be afraid if you don't know any words in Italian. Most people can understand English, and even if they don't speak it fluently, they will do their best to make you understand what they want to say. Probably by gesturing.

As you know, we Italians are great gesticulators. You will probably be able to understand what two people are saying to each other by the way they communicate. Even if you don't speak Italian!

In general, we love tourists and are always willing to give guidance.

If you need extra info or assistance, pop in to the "Ufficio IAT Informazioni e Accoglienza Turistiche".

It is right in the city centre in Via Degli Alpini, next to Piazza Bra, inside the old medieval city walls.

It is used by both tourists and locals who want to stay up-to-date. It offers a huge number of brochures and leaflets on museums, monuments and churches, cultural events, practical information about car parking and bus timetables, and much, much more. They speak amazingly good English!

# 6. "VERONESI TUTTI MATTI' (VERONESI ARE ALL MAD)

There is a rhyme, known throughout northern Italy, which goes 'Veneziani gran signori, padovani gran dottori, veronesi tutti matti e vicentini magna gatti'. Venetians great lords, Paduans great doctors, Veronese all mad and Vicentines eat cats.

Well. In Venice, they were rich. Padua is famous for its university. Vicentini, cat eaters, well... poverty was widespread in the area. I hate that too.

Let's get to it: the Veronesi, crazy people. It's not super clear.

Some say it is because of the delicious red wine. In 568 A.D. a certain Theodoric recommended the consumption of typical wine (recioto) for its "fleshy liquid, a drink to eat" capable of... invigorating the spirit.

Some say it is for the Carnival festival, particularly the Gnocolar Friday parade, where songs, dances and madness fill every street.

Some say that it is Verona's innumerable churches that tempt its inhabitants to get up to all sorts of mischief. There are so many churches, it is so easy to ask for forgiveness!

However, it is Goethe's words (on his trip to Italy in 1786) that best render that 'tutti matti' (all mad). He mentions it when describing Piazza Erbe, which has always been the centre of Veronese life.

"On market days, the crowd in the square is huge, and the eye can be delighted by the sight of mountains of fruit, vegetables, garlic, onions. Everyone shouts, sings, jokes all throughout the day; they push each other, bump into each other, make a fuss and laugh all the time...'.

That's my favourite explanation.

# 7. I GET AROUND (ROUND, GET AROUND–ROUND–ROUND, OOH) (WAH–WAH–OOH)

*I Get Around*, The Beach Boys. Thank me later.

Getting around in Verona is easy, quick, and usually eco-friendly.

Verona is very small and dense, so you can reach all the main points of interest easily. Leave your car outside the city centre and have a walk or get around by bus or bike.

Why no car? Well, it's not forbidden. However, consider that the

majority of the city centre is a restricted traffic area (look for the "ZTL"

sign). This means that is closed to normal vehicles apart from residents,

hotel guests and deliveries during specific time periods.

# 8. COMING BY CAR

Coming to Verona by car? Time to find a spot to park it and enjoy your walk.

You can park your vehicle in a covered car park (charges apply) close to the city centre, or choose one of the free car parks, unsupervised and a little further from the city centre but reachable either by walking or by bus.

Best covered one is Parcheggio Arena. My favourite free ones are Parcheggio Porta Palio (V.le Galliano/Stradone Porta Palio), Parcheggio Piazzale Guardini, and Parcheggio Libero Don Mazza.

# 9. YOUR BEST OPTIONS: BUS AND BIKE

The buses run from around 5 am to midnight. Tickets can be purchased online using the Ticket Bus Verona app, from retailers or from the shops called Tabacchi.

Look out for these big T signs!

Tabacchi sign from Pixabay.com.

Tickets are valid for 90 minutes. Day tickets are also available, and also books of 10 tickets which are better value than buying individual tickets.

Consider purchasing the Verona Card, so along with travelling for free on local buses, you get free or reduced admission to the main museums, monuments, and churches in the city.

My favourite travelling method, however, is by bike. Find one of the many bike and e-bike hire outlets in the city or try the Verona Bike service. Verona Bike is available online at bikeverona.it for a daily fee of only €2, €5 for a week or €10 for a month. (I'll say it again: only 10€ per month!). Plus, the first half-hour of use is always free of charge. Amazing!

# 10. YOUR CAFFEINE FIX, THE ITALIAN WAY

You've made it! You're ready to start your journey to the land of stunning monuments, dreamy landscapes, gorgeous art, crystal clear water... and lots of delicious food. Let's face it, this is the first thing you think of when you hear about Italy.

The next few paragraphs will be dedicated to the food and culinary traditions of this country. Because yeah, if it's true that you can (and should!) enjoy any kind of food at any time, don't be surprised if we recognize you as a tourist when you're having a cappuccino paired with a slice of pizza at 4 p.m. (I'm looking at you, German people.)

Let's start with coffee. For us, it is a sacred moment. The tradition is to have an espresso in a small, very hot cup, mostly straight at the counter. Italian espresso is strong, effective, and extremely practical and quick. The aim is just to ingest caffeine (with a fantastic taste). It costs €1 at the bar, €1.30 served at the table.

Please note: if you ask for a "caffè lungo", long coffee, you will not get an Americano! You will get an espresso with an extra teaspoon of water. Be prepared, the big cup of coffee typical of the movies does not exist here.

Anyway! To ensure you avoid odd looks from Italians puzzled by your food choices, the next paragraphs are dedicated to the meals and snacks culture in Italy, and more specifically, to the best that my city has to offer. (Winks at the Spritz at 2.5€)

# 11. SWEET BREAKFAST – "CAPPUCCINO AND BRIOCHE".

Buongiorno! To start the day in the best way, Italians usually have a sweet breakfast. It is the most important meal of the day, and we load up on energy. An old popular saying of ours goes "Breakfast like a king, lunch like a prince, dinner like a peasant".

The most popular breakfast is milk and biscuits/cookies (if you're in Italy, you shouldn't leave without a box of Mulino Bianco biscuits). The typical Italian breakfast, in any case, consists of milk, coffee, rusks, jam, yogurt and orange juice. There are millions of variations that do not affect the overall package: tea instead of coffee, toast instead of rusks, honey instead of jam, fresh fruit for the yogurt.

A common choice is also 'colazione al bar', breakfast at a bar, perhaps with friends or colleagues. When the first meal of the day is eaten outside the home, the choice is one: cappuccino and croissant. (Bonus point if the barista makes drawings on the cappuccino foam).

Please note: Cappuccino in Italy is a breakfast drink. Usually, having one after 11 am is a bit strange. Especially when paired with a pizza or pasta dish.

# 12. LUNCHTIME: I CAN SENSE THE PASTA APPROACHING

As 12pm approaches, Italians are already thinking about the pasta dish that awaits them. This is the best moment to try the Italian kitchen. There are so many possibilities, you can probably eat somewhere different every day and never eat the same dish twice!

Lunch in Italy is usually between 12.30 and 2 pm, and consists of a first course (a pasta, risotto or soup), the second course of meat or fish with vegetables, and fruit, a dessert or coffee.

Most restaurants close their kitchen at around 2.30 p.m. so you can't really have a full lunch later than that. Bars, however, are open full day.

People with little time, such as workers, university students or busy tourists, eat a sandwich, a tramezzino, a delicious piadina at a bar and then go straight back to business.

# 13. WHERE TO HAVE LUNCH

My advice for a nutritious and inexpensive lunch is to go for "osteria" or "trattoria", specifically the ones where you can find a "pranzo di lavoro", "worker's lunch". This menu is for local workers who usually have a short lunch break, a big appetite and little money to spend. You will find a delicious two-course meal, plus water and coffee at no more than 13€. And you will leave the table with a full belly.

Around the city, however, there are plenty of delicious little eateries. Some fresh pasta shops have better reviews than the Michelin restaurants in town! When in doubt, choose local. My advice for fresh pasta: try "La Vecia Mescola Dell'Oste".

# 14. MERENDINA (SNACKS)

Around 4 or 5 pm, when you feel a little peckish, it's time for the "merenda". I used to think it was an international thing, but I have discovered while writing this book that it is a uniquely Italian prerogative!

In our country, the afternoon snack is considered - to all intents and purposes - a meal, albeit a small one compared to the two others. The Italians' top five snacks include fruit, pastry, yogurt, salty snacks, small sandwiches with bread and salami. It is often combined with coffee or hot tea.

This is the children's favourite moment because for them Merenda usually means bread and Nutella! I had to put that in writing, but it's not actually just for children... *winks*

# 15. THE SACRED APERITIVO

"Let's meet for an aperitivo" is one of the most beautiful love phrases in the world.

Joking aside, Verona is the city of love but also the city of the aperitivo. Let's say... love for the aperitivo.

The aperitivo is something that we, as Italians, deeply love. It is served in bars and wineries from 17.30 to 19.30, the time when work is over. People gather with colleagues, friends and relatives, and enjoy a delicious drink together.

One of the most popular aperitifs in Italy is the Spritz, which can be mixed with Aperol or Campari, ice and a slice of orange (not lemon!).

And I'm very happy you'll be in Verona. This is the "land of the Spritz", where the best ones are served at a really cheap price, usually from 2,5€ to 3,50€. Try it yourself, we are very proud of it.

Other drinks include Prosecco for the more refined palate, Soave, and cocktails such as Americano, Hugo, Negroni and so on, to suit all tastes.

The aperitif is usually served with some appetizers, such as chips, olives, peanuts and, if you are in the right place, a "tagliere di affettati". I'll talk about this later in typical foods!

# 16. MORE ABOUT APERITIVO (AND WHERE TO HAVE IT)

The aperitif has evolved over the years and the tendency is to make it longer so that it incorporates dinner as well. Some places now offer the apericena, cheaper than a dinner and much more filling than a simple aperitivo. (around 10€ with a drink of your choice).

Want insider tips? Try these places: Osteria del Bugiardo, in Corso Porta Borsari 17, where you will have a quintessential Veronese aperitif with lots of typical products like cheese and salami. Other places not to be missed are La Tradision, Via Guglielmo Oberdan, 6, and Rivamancina, Vicolo Quadrelli, 1, where you can enjoy a delicious aperitif while admiring the river.

Later in the evening, Piazza Delle Erbe contains the fixed stop: Mazzanti, with its "aperitivo vetrina". A reference point for Veronese nightlife.

# 17. DINNER TIME IN ITALY

We Italians love dinner. It's the best time at the end of the day when all family members and friends gather around the table and have a meal while talking about the most important events. At dinner, we usually eat lighter food such as cold cuts, fish, cheese and vegetables. You can have dinner from 7 p.m to 9 p.m. (10 p.m. in summer) and it's usually the longest of meals.

When it comes to dinner, the possibilities are endless in Verona! The city is full of cosy little restaurants and even if you pick one with your eyes closed, I'm sure you'd be pleased.

I will share with you a couple of places that are hidden from the tourist radar: Enoteca Segreta, in Vicolo Samaritana, 10, small and hidden by many alleys. Prices are a bit above average, but it's worth it, especially for a romantic dinner.

Ristorante Arche is suitable for outings with friends: adored by locals, it offers more affordable prices and makes a risotto all'Amarone that is nothing short of dreamy. Try it for yourself. A similar one tucked away in a quiet side street away from tourists, is Enocibus: traditional dishes based on simple products, risottos and kinds of pasta, at very affordable prices, in Vicolo Pomodoro, 3.

Finally, my favourite. They don't take reservations but will do everything to serve you: Osteria Sottoriva, at Via Sottoriva 9, is one of the most famous eateries, popular for its quality food and affordable prices. Do not choose this place for a quick meal: there's a sign at the entrance warning "slow service"!

After dinner, enjoy the rest that the night has to offer as you walk through the centre's various wineries and bars.

# 18. WHAT TO EAT – TYPICAL VERONA FOODS

I am going to focus for a moment on the typical foods of Verona, those that marked my childhood and that make my taste buds rejoice every single time. Hopefully I will be able to fully express the enthusiasm I feel for these dishes, and they may become your favourites too!

All the recipes make creative and delicious dishes from simple ingredients. Below are 5 typical dishes that you should not miss.

# 19. MUST TRY: RISOTTO ALL'AMARONE AND POLENTA

Risotto all'amarone is one of the most typical and universally loved Veronese dishes. It combines all the territory's most renowned ingredients: Vialone Nano rice, grown in the Veronese lowlands. Amarone Della Valpolicella, one of the finest red wines in Italy. Grated Monte Veronese, a cheese produced only in the area. This combo is simply spectacular.

The second dish is that yellow thing typical of the Veronese area, you'll find it on your plate together with mushrooms, salami and cheese. It's polenta, usually made with corn flour and other mysterious ingredients.

# 20. BIGOLI: WE TOOK SPAGHETTI AND MADE IT BETTER

Bigoli is a typical Veronese pasta very similar to spaghetti, but thicker and denser. I grew up eating bigoli, and when, at the ripe old age of 14-15 years old, I ordered spaghetti in a restaurant for the first time, I was disappointed by that strange, thin thing.

# 21. RISOTTO WITH TASTASAL

Among the dishes of typical Veronese cuisine, another risotto stands out, namely risotto with tastasal (a type of minced pork meat). Accompany it with fine Veronese wines such as Bardolino or Valpolicella and you'll remember it forever.

# 22. PANDORO (OUR DESSERT WITH A PATENT) AND THE COMPETITION WITH PANETTONE

A gem of sweetness made with flour, brewer's yeast, sugar, butter, eggs, vanilla and, to enhance everything, icing sugar. Here, as you see, there are no candied fruits or creams. (Picture me looking askance at the rival panettone, a typical Milanese dessert). Our original recipe is sober, elegant. Leavened, very soft and without any crust.

It is easy to read, but not so easy to prepare: you need up to 36 hours, with at least 10 hours of rising and 7 cycles of kneading.

It originates from 'pane de oro', (bread made of gold), a delicacy served on the tables of Venetian nobles. Today we don't know the precise roots of pandoro, but there is no doubt at all about how it should be.

The inventor of the pandoro is Domenico Melegatti. In 1884 he presented the patent for this Christmas cake which was immediately loved first by the Veronese, then by the whole world. (And it tastes better than Panettone, with which we are in open competition). Pandoro and Panettone are the classic desserts that are found on the tables of Italians at Christmas time, and which for years have opened up feuds, competitions and fights to the death at Christmas dinners.

In Verona, we love pandoro so much that we made a statue of it! It's not easy to spot though. Find it out in the section on Verona's secret places later on this book.

Ps: I'm moving abroad for a while. I plan to take at least 4 Pandoro with me. I'm not joking.

# 23. HAVE 'FRITOLE'

Another dessert on my list, Fritole (small fritters) have been proclaimed the national dessert of the Veneto State. I'll let you find out by yourself why.

PS: make sure you get the typical Veronese ones.

# 24. TRY "TAGLIERE DI AFFETTATI"

It is an Italian tradition that the best meals (or aperitifs) begin with a good board of cold cuts, sliced meats and cheeses. Its presence on the table makes a relaxed and sharing atmosphere. People chat and laugh while they taste the delicacies in front of them, experimenting with various combinations. Being able to create a balanced board is trivial, and bonus points for the aesthetics of the dish too.

In Verona, you should really stop and enjoy a good tagliere. Insider tips: Trattoria Al Pompiere, perhaps one of the best restaurants in Verona. Hidden away at the beginning of Via Cappello, here you'll find thirty-five different types of cold cuts and a hundred different types of cheese. Impossible to resist.

Between Ponte Nuovo and via Sottoriva, there is also Il Banco, a prosciutteria with a magical atmosphere of industrial design and ancient vaults.

# 25. WHEN TO VISIT VERONA

The city is beautiful all year round, but each season has its own reasons for choosing it.

In summer the heat can be really intense, but this is the perfect season if you'd like to enjoy a show at the Arena or in the splendid Roman Amphitheatre. In winter, on the other hand, the city of love shows its best version, first for the Christmas markets and then for Valentine's Day.

In spring it slowly awakens and begins to fill up with the early tourists. The soft rays of the sun bring everyone out of their homes for their first weekends away, maybe at the lake or the nearby hills.

In autumn, finally, people cosy up in their homes and offices, there are few tourists, especially on the coldest days, and everything calms down. It is splendid: it's you, the city and those who have some errands to do. There are cities that in this season, with the sky turning grey, switch off, while Verona, on the other hand, only dims its lights, achieving a magical autumnal atmosphere. This is why, in my opinion, it is the best season to visit, perhaps between the end of September and October. And also Piazza Erbe begins to smell like roasted chestnuts.

## 26. "A VACATION IS A SUNBURN AT PREMIUM PRICES." – HAL CHADWICKE

One thing you can never go without when travelling to Verona, is sunscreen. Spring, summer and early autumn make sure you have with you a hat and a bottle of sunscreen. It's not that hot, but the sunshine is enough to get you. As much as I love seeing reddish tourists admiring the wonders of my city, your nose and the back of your neck will thank me later. At the end of the day, don't forget you are in "sunny Italy".

# 27. CAN YOU VISIT VERONA IN ONE DAY?

Yes! One day is just enough to see the main attractions. I've already mentioned earlier that the historic centre is small and dense, and can be explored entirely on foot or by bike. (It's best to walk, so you can get homemade ice cream and eat it on the way. Or a mulled wine if it's winter).

Of course, as always with art cities, the more time you have, the more you can discover all its nuances and peculiarities.

The next paragraphs are dedicated to the main attractions that my city has to offer and that you should not miss. I will then dwell on the less known and locals' favourite places!

# 28. A VERY SHORT AND SUPER INTERESTING HISTORY OF VERONA (JUST ENOUGH TO SHOW YOU KNOW)

Yadda yadda, the area around Verona has been inhabited since the Neolithic period and has welcomed many different peoples until 49 BC, when the city became a Roman municipality under the name Res Publica Veronensium.

In the beginning, it was located in the current area of Colle San Pietro (today a nice walk from which you can enjoy a stunning view, more on that later), but the Romans moved its historical centre to the one you are going to visit. The centre is full of relics from the era, first and foremost the Arena, but also other gems such as the Roman Subway Arch with its original stones. (Yes, that's not its real name).

Other important names to show you know? After the fall of the Roman Empire in 476 AD, Verona became ruled by Theodoric the Great. A figure adored by the Veronese, he transformed Verona into one of the most important centres of his kingdom.

Passing from hand to hand between local kingdoms until 1136, Verona was marked by internal struggles between the Guelphs and Ghibellines, the latter led by the Montecchi. (The rivalry with the Montecchi of Vicenza is still in force today!)

The name sounds familiar? Juliet was a Veronese, Romeo was a Montecchio. These are the real foundations of Shakespeare's story.

Another important name: Cangrande I della Scala, who, along with leading the city and the surrounding towns of Vicenza, Padua and Belluno into a period of immense splendour, welcomed the famous poet Dante to Verona. He was exiled from his city, Florence. Dante dedicated the entire canticle of Paradise in The Divine Comedy to Cangrande of Verona! The Veronese are slightly proud of this.

Bad things: plague in 1630. French (Napoleon's troops) in 1796. We are still mad at the French people because, in the Napoleonic spoliation of Verona, many works of art were taken to the Louvre Museum in Paris and *are still there.*

The city was first French and then Austrian territory, and was finally incorporated into the

Kingdom of Italy on 16 October 1866. Since then its history has been intertwined with that of the rest of the peninsula.

# 29. VISIT THE ARENA OF VERONA (FINALLY!)

Yes, it's probably the first thing you want to see once you arrive in Verona. You can't say Verona without saying arena (well, yes, almost).

Verona is the Arena. Its circular structure welcomes you as soon as you arrive in the city, it stands out in front of you when you get to the end of Via Mazzini and find yourself in Piazza Bra. It is full of memories from the past (it has been here since the first century AD!), emotions, stories enclosed in every single stone.

During the summer it is an open-air theatre of emotions, music and shows. It makes the square vibrate to the rhythm of music, from rock concerts to pop, to the world-famous Opera. At this time of year, the city is filled with people in luxurious jackets and evening dresses. In winter, however, it is where the veronese comet starts - it lights up Piazza Bra during the Christmas markets. (Have a look at some photos!)

From the outside it's magnificent, but if it's your first time in the city, it's worth going inside and climbing to the top to see the whole square from above. If it's Christmas time, there will be an exhibition of nativity scenes. (note: you need a ticket to get in!).

If you're lucky, you might find the huge sets used for the shows right outside the Arena. They are put out there before moving them to another place. Personally, I love it so much. You walk through the centre and find yourself in front of a giant sphinx! Everyday stuff.

## 30. TOUCH LE TETTE DI GIULIETTA – (YES THAT MEANS BOOBS)

You will know you have arrived when you find yourself in front of a huge amount of tourists standing in the middle of a street.

Juliet's house, with its letters written on the walls, lovers' padlocks attached to every single metal clasp and its messages of hope, gratitude and sorrow, is one of the most romantic and beloved places in the city.

It is a small house with an inner courtyard, and inside of it is the bronze statue of Juliet. As per tradition, put your hand on her right breast (it's worn out by now!) in the hope that it will bring luck in love (you know, she had a really happy love story...)

From the inner courtyard, you can see Juliet's balcony, and you can get inside the actual house with a ticket. There are furnishings, objects of the era and costumes. I recommend it if you want a bit of extra romance in your holiday or if you particularly like Shakespeare's story.

# 31. OBVIOUSLY, GO SHOPPING (IN VIA MAZZINI)

There is a large number of high-fashion shops in Verona, especially in the famous Via Mazzini, the street that connects Piazza Bra with Piazza Delle Erbe. absolute shopping street, a favourite for tourists and locals alike. There are many brands here, ranging

49

from Armani to Gucci, Coco Chanel to Dolce and Gabbana, but there are also smaller, more traditional boutiques.

The shops are open every day and you can stroll around admiring the windows and buying yourself a gift to commemorate this fantastic trip.

PS: Via Mazzini hides a fascinating secret corner. I will mention it the next sections.

# 32. WALK AROUND PIAZZA DELLE ERBE (ONE OF THE MOST BEAUTIFUL SQUARES IN ITALY!)

I take it for granted that you have already seen Piazza Bra on your way to the Arena di Verona. Piazza Erbe is the secondary square, the one I actually prefer. Smaller, more intimate, it is the heart of the ancient city and is always full of stalls selling touristy things. At Christmas time it's beautiful: there are lots of cascading lights and a giant Christmas tree.

If you're like me and love all things Christmasy, the Christmas Markets in Piazza Delle Erbe in Verona is definitely the place to be during the festive season.

# 33. CONSIDER GOING UP TO TORRE DEI LAMBERTI (SOME STEPS!)

You're already in Piazza Erbe, so you can't fail to stop and admire the Lamberti Tower. Built in the 12th century, it has been above Piazza Erbe since 1469! It is the highest tower in the city, and its 85 metres will let you have a spectacular view over the whole Verona - it will literally be at your feet! At the time, the lords of Verona competed to see who had the tallest tower. The Lamberti Tower is the only one remaining today, and it is well worth a visit. And a reward in the form of an ice cream after climbing all those steps.

Local insight: its two bells were used to communicate with the citizens, with a special code. Rengo, the larger bell, used to convene the Town Council or important meetings, while Marangona, the smaller one, used to warn of fires!

51

# 34. DEFINITELY GO UP TO CASTEL SAN PIETRO (SOME MORE STEPS!)

Okay, Castel San Pietro is beautiful, full stop. And before you say anything about the number of steps it takes to get to the top, let me assure you that it's well worth it. Especially if you climb up with someone you love. (Shared suffering improves the relationship, right?).

From the magnificent Ponte Pietra to a panoramic terrace at the top of Castel San Pietro, it's a truly wonderful walk with a breathtaking view of Verona. Best of all, visit during the sunset hours, with the soft light and the first lights of the city on.

I didn't want to tell you, but you can also go up by funicular. It's about 3€ one way or 5€ return.

To maximize your walk, get a delicious gelato at Gelateria Ponte Pietra, one of the best in Verona, right before you cross the bridge and start going up. You'll thank me later.

# 35. GO FIND OUT WHY I LOVE CASTELVECCHIO SO MUCH

Castelvecchio: yadda yadda, one of the city's main historical sites. World War II, bombings and renovations, it now houses a museum dedicated mainly to medieval art, with paintings, sculptures, archaeological finds and ancient weapons.

The thing is, it is stunning. It's one of my favourite places in the city. I love the path you walk through over the river, absolutely beautiful. The Castelvecchio Bridge is massive and has imposing walls that you can sort of climb. It leads to a little park with benches where you can have a picnic or just ice cream (yes, me and my ice cream passion).

Eventually, if you go on the left after crossing the bridge and follow the river, you can go touch the water, throw some stones or, if you're lucky, feed some ducks. They are so cute.

Castelvecchio in the evening, with the city lights reflecting on the Adige, is a view you shouldn't miss out on.

Do you plan to travel in the summer? Bring flip flops! The little park at the end of the bridge has a small square that is filled with water when the summer season begins. You can go dip your toes in and dance in the water.

# 36. LESS KNOWN PLACES IN VERONA

Verona is full of corners, narrow streets, places that don't fall under the tourist radar and are often populated mostly by the locals. Let me give you a list!

Verona is known for Juliet's balcony, but only a few people know that there is also Juliet's tomb, the church of Juliet and Romeo's wedding, and Romeo's house!

The famous Juliet's house was the home of the Capulet family, presumed to be Juliet's house, and tourists flock to take pictures on the balcony and with Juliet's statue in the courtyard.

The house of Romeo Montecchi instead is located in Via Arche Scaligere, 2-4: it is a massive medieval palace in the centre of Verona, with high crenellated walls that make it look like a small castle. Since it is now a private house, it cannot be visited, but it's worth a stop right after Juliet's house. If you walk along the shortest route, it is probably the same route Romeo used to run to get to Juliet.

There is also a hidden crypt inside the church of the Balisica di San Zeno. It's underground, small and secret: here the marriage between Romeo and Juliet has been celebrated. This intimate and romantic dungeon is as hidden as the love of the two protagonists.

Juliet's tomb is located in the former convent of San Francesco al Corso. It doesn't get so many tourists visits.

# 37. THE ARCHE SCALIGERE AND THE MOVABLE GATE

Just behind Piazza Erbe and Piazza Dante, in the shadow of the Torre Dei Lamberti (the one we mentioned earlier) are the Arche Scaligere, tombs of the Della Scala lords. They ruled Verona in the thirteenth and fourteenth centuries. Their canopied tombs are exceptional monuments that are well visible from the street, inside an ornate wrought-iron gate,

What not everyone knows is that part of the wrought iron gate, which features the family symbol, is movable. The movable gate is the original one, the parts made in more recent times are fixed instead. Try to move them and find out.

Arche scaligere picture from Pixabay.com

# 38. GO SHOPPING IN THE MIDDLE OF ROMAN RUINS (LITERALLY!)

Via Mazzini is the fashion shopping street and the main street of the historic centre. But you would not expect the two to match, and to find Roman remains in the middle of a fashion store! In Benetton's basement, however, this is very much possible. Try going downstairs and having a look for yourself. The remains of a Roman villa are perfectly preserved among modern designer clothes.

# 39. THE SECRET WELL OF LOVERS (NO, NOT ROMEO AND JULIET)

Verona is full of hidden fun and love stories! It's not just Romeo and Juliet, although they are the tourist's favourite.

Hidden among the narrow streets, houses and courtyards, there is a secret well, the only thing left of the love between Corrado di San Bonifazio and Isabella Donati, a young soldier and a lady of the 16th century. According to the legend, Corrado was in love with the lady, but she was reluctant to show her feelings.

One day the two met near this well. He, sad and tired, told Isabella that she seemed to him as cold as the water in that well.

The girl told him to jump in and see if the water was as actually as cold as he thought. Corrado, desperate, jumped in. Isabella, out of love for him, jumped into the well too, disappearing with him. Happy love stories aren't the norm in this city, apparently.

It is a secret because it's not so easy to reach. Once you arrive to Corso Porta Borsari, go ahead until house number 15 and turn left into Vicolo San Marco in Foro. After a few metres, on the left, there is a narrow alley called Pozzo (Well) San Marco. Here you will find the well.

# 40. CHALLENGE SOMEONE TO SPOT THE CREATOR OF ARCH OF THE GAVI (OR THE SUBWAY ARCH). ADMIRE THE ORIGINAL ROMAN STONES UNDERNEATH!

A must-see, literally right next to Castelvecchio, the Arch of the Gavi shines in white stone and with a history of its own. It was, in fact, once placed somewhere else.

During the period of Napoleonic power in Italy, French people demolished the Arch. Its ruins were saved by the Veronese, including the Roman street stones underneath it. Some decades later it has been put back on its feet in a different, more convenient location. What you see now are indeed the original stones from when it was built. We're talking about stones of Roman origin! People with togas and sandals used to walk on top of that road. Look closely: they even have the signs of Roman chariots.

Today the arch is also called the Subway Arch because the shop is just a little further on the road. It is a tradition for us Veronese people to get a sandwich and sit under the arch to eat, enjoying the magnificent view of the river.

The monument was designed by an architect who successfully left *winks* his signature for posterity. His name, Lucius Vitruvius (L.VITRVIVS L.L. CERDO ARCHITECTVS), is in fact engraved on one of the stone blocks. Try to find out which one.

# 41. WE LOVE PANDORO SO MUCH THAT WE MADE A STATUE OF IT. OR MAYBE TWO.

We have already talked about the unquestionable superiority of Pandoro, the typical dessert of Verona. Try to spot the two Pandoro statues at number 21 of Corso Porta Borsari.

Hint: look up at the terraces on the fourth floor. It is no coincidence that this building once housed the pastry shop of Domenico Melegatti, the inventor of our favourite dessert, so leavened, soft and crustless.

# 42. LEARN SOME PHRASES – LANGUAGE BASICS

Now that we have seen what you should visit and try in the city, here are some phrases you can use to communicate better. I already mentioned that most Italians understand English and will try their best to speak it. Making an effort to speak Italian is not strictly necessary, but it will be deeply appreciated. And you may get involved in experiences that would not have been possible if you had been speaking only English!

# 43. WE ACTUALLY SAY MAMMA MIA

Yes, we do say "Mamma mia". It is used when we want to emphasize our excitement or wonder about something. It has meanings from "dang you look amazing!!" to "holy sh—!" or even "wtf?!" and "OMG!". To be honest, it is usually said when swearing is not appropriate. (Otherwise, you will be treated to a delightfully colourful swear expression.)

Another useful expression is Cin cin (or Salute).

When doing a toast, at the moment when the glasses touch each other, we Italians have two options: a shouted SALUTEEE or a cute "cin-cin", according to the room mood. Cin cin is the same sound that the glasses make when they touch each other. It's always adorable to see a group of people together all going "cin cin" with glasses in their hands.

# 44. UNA PIZZA, PER FAVORE (OONA PEE-SA PEHR FA - VOH - REH)

For real tho, let's get started with the common Italian phrases and words that will be most useful to you on your travels. I tried to write down the easiest phonetic pronunciation as well, so you get a vague idea of how words are supposed to sound.

English - Italian - Pronunciation:

Yes - Sì - See

No – No – Noh. (This one can also be said with a click of your mouth sound. Check that in the next chapter.)

Please – Per favore – Pehr fah-voh-reh

Thank you – Grazie – Grah-tsee-eh

Hi / Bye – Ciao! – Cheeao

Good morning – Buon giorno – Bwohn-johr-noh

Good bye – Arrivederci – Ahr-ree-veh-dehr-chee (this one wasn't easy to write down)

Cheers! – Salute! – Sah-loo-tay (or Cin cin!)

Excuse me (for attention) – Scusi – Skooh–ze

Excuse me (to pass by) – Permesso – Pehr-mehs-soh

I don't understand – Non capisco – Non kah-pee-skoh

I'm sorry – Mi dispiace – Mee dees-pyah-cheh

Useful as well:

House wine – Vino della casa – Vee-noh del-lah car-sah

# 45. THE TRUE WAY TO SPEAK ITALIAN: HAND GESTURES (YES, YOU'LL NEED A GUIDE)

You are in Italy, where your voice itself is not enough to communicate. Here, expressing yourself is done through gestures, and sometimes without even uttering a word. Learn to gesture like a real Italian with me.

Another way of saying no: click of your mouth + index finger moving sideways. Try looking it up on Youtube. This is the answer most Italians give to "yes or no questions" and many foregneirs are left confused at the Italian person in front of them suddenly lagging.

Ahh, yes. Put all of your fingers together and move your hand up and down. This classical Italian gesture means wtf or "hell no".

Rub your thumb, first and middle finger together. What did you want for Christmas, again? This gesture means "money".

## 46. "CONO OR COPPETTA?" BEST GELATERIA IN VERONA

You'll hear this phrase a lot if you go for ice cream (as you should) when in Verona. It means: "cup or cone?"

I have a hilarious anecdote about this. Once a friend of mine was determined to learn Italian, he decided he would only speak Italian in a day in Verona with me.

It was time to have ice cream together (at this point of the book you already got it that I love ice cream), and he wanted to order. Using an artificial translator, he translated the word "a cup" into the Italian equivalent of flower pot. (Vaso instead of coppetta). He ordered, literally, "a pot of ice cream".

The ice cream lady didn't flinch for a second. With extreme seriousness, she took the flower pot with all the daisies in the window shop, and handing it to him, asked if that size would be okay for him.

My friend was puzzled at first, but once he realised the mistake, didn't stop laughing for the rest of the day.


I promised it to you, and here I am, revealing to you the best ice-cream shop in Verona.

Well, there are actually a lot of them...

When in doubt, always check that they are artisanal, staying away from windows with bright colour ice cream and excessive amounts of it on display. They are probably full of colouring agents and are industrially made.

Top 3 are: Gelateria Ponte Pietra (before Ponte Pietra eheh), The art of ice cream in Via Leoni, 3 and Gelateria La Romana, in Piazza Santo Spirito, 9.

# 47. WHAT SOUVENIRS TO BRING HOME? BUY SOME GROCERIES (YOUR BEST OPTION).

Verona is steeped in craftsmanship and passion for quality. Take home a slice of Verona in the form of excellently made products (whether you will eat them or not).

The historic centre of Verona is an ideal destination for travellers who like to lose themselves in artisan boutiques, little local shops, eateries and wineries.

My advice is to opt for a tasty souvenir: from the supermarket to local shops, you can easily find typical products at great convenience. The local specialities are obviously cheeses, cured meats, pasta dishes, desserts and wines, but there are also truffles, mushrooms and olives. And don't forget to get yourself a nice pack of good pasta, which costs very little here. And a Pandoro.

For the best artisanal and "homemade" food, I recommend La Botteghetta, in Via Leoncino 31. This typical Veronese family-run delicatessen offers cold meats, cheeses, focaccia, breadsticks and much more. Here the shopkeeper is both knowledgeable and enthusiastic, with a clear passion for what he sells. He will relentlessly hunt for the ideal cheese for you, making you do thousands of tastings. Imagine Olivander from Harry Potter, but with more cheese.

Another insider choice is the Gastronomia di Via Stella, which not only has great quality products but also offers a good aperitif right there, with fresh produce.

My tip: ask to try the Amarone cheese!

# 48. JOIN THE LOCALS AT THE WEEKLY MARKET

And finally, if you want to enjoy the most genuine aspect the city has to offer, you absolutely have to pop in the weekly market.

The one in Corso Porta Nuova is held every Friday morning from 8 am to 2 pm, with the various stalls filling the whole avenue up to the main square. It is populated by real locals: neighbourhood residents, grandparents, students, children holding hands with their parents, typical Veronese people. They come here to buy everything, from clothes and typical products to household utensils, fruit and vegetables.

Local farmers sell their products here coming straight from their farmhouses, such as fruit, vegetables, meats, cheese and wine. This is the real "km 0"!

I really recommend paying a visit to the market, especially if you want to find some deals. The prices are really convenient here compared to shops, for good quality products. Whether you need to fill your pantry, you are looking for deals or just want to spend the morning surrounded by scents and bright colours, the market is the place to be.

Ps: there is a stall selling super soft sweaters at the beginning of Corso Porta Nuova and I can't help buying a new one every winter.

# 49. EXTRA TIME? DAY VISIT TO LAKE GARDA

Verona is surprisingly well connected: from here you can reach by car or train other cities of art such as Vicenza, Padua, Mantua, Brescia or Bologna. Trentino and Alto Adige are close by and there are connections to the major Italian and European cycle routes.

The city is also just a few kilometres from the Lessini mountains (where the good wine is eheh) and Lake Garda.

These two are fantastic options if you have a day to spare! From Verona you can reach the lake by train: from Porta Nuova station, get off at Peschiera del Garda. The journey takes about a quarter of an hour! Plus the prices are very affordable, starting from less than 4 euros for the regional train.

You can also go by bus, from the same station, and in this case, you can take your bike with you. I really recommend it, biking along the lake and having a picnic by the shore is my favourite thing to do. It's always a great idea for a day out and requires minimal preparation.

# 50. GODITI A PIENO LA TUA VACANZA!

I know I've said it before, but I've travelled to many different countries, tried different cuisines and met a lot of wonderful people on my travels, but nothing compares to the beauty of Italy and the warmth of its people.

This year in particular there have been more worries than there should have been. It is finally your time to fully enjoy at the fullest the landscapes, the art, the food, the history and the genuine people who live on this peninsula. I truly believe Italy is an unmissable destination, and one lifetime is not enough to enjoy all the beauty enclosed here. Live fully every second of your Italian holiday and it will make you smile every time you think about it.

I hope my tips will be useful to you during your holiday in Verona, and I hope to see you around! Whatever you decide to do, it is your time to do something out of the ordinary and it doesn't matter if it lasts a day, just a couple of hours or a week, your aim is to create pleasant memories that make you feel good.

Benvenuto in Italia!

# TOP REASONS TO BOOK THIS TRIP

You will fall in Love: Verona is the city of Love, from the famous Romeo and Juliet's passion to the pure joy and amazement you will feel seeing all the monuments, landscapes and art the city has to offer. Due to its beauty, Verona is a UNESCO gem from 2000!

Food: The food is amazing. The most prestigious wines and cheeses of Italy are made here, and you can enjoy a delicious Spritz with snacks at only 2.50€.

Italian Culture: you can merge with the locals in this amazing little town and live like a true Italian, enjoying your life to the fullest in every single moment. Have a brioche al bar in the early morning, walk down the sunny and populated streets during the afternoon, create and share memories with all your friends and family in front of a good meal and drink at the end of the day.

# TRIVIA

1) What does the shape of Italy remind of?

2) What is the surname of Juliet? And the one of Romeo?

3) Where can you go shopping underground in the middle of the remains of a Roman villa?

4) Why is Pandoro better than Panettone?

5) How do you call the small coins and change in Italian?

6) What is the fruity ingredient of the delicious Spritz? Lemon or orange?

7) What is the other way Italian people say "no"?

8) What does "cin-cin" mean?

9) Why do you need flip flops to visit Castelvecchio during the summer sesason?

10) Should you touch le Tette di Giulietta?

# ANSWERS

1) A Boot With A Heel.
2) Giulietta Capuleti and Romeo Montecchi!
3) In Via Mazzini, the Benetton store has an underground Villa Romana.
4) Because it's simple, but elegant, soft and delicious. Flour, brewer's yeast, sugar, butter, eggs, vanilla. Here, as you see, there are no candied fruits or creams to ruin the whole thing. Plus you need up to 36 hours to make it, with at least 10 hours of rising and 7 cycles of kneading. Amazing.
5) Monetine. And you use them to pay for your Espresso!
6) The ingredients are: Prosecco, Campari or Aperol, Sparkling water, Ice and a... orange slice.
7) They click with the tongue and move the index finger.
8) It's one of the expressions Italians use for Cheers!
9) Because the little square there gets filled with water and you can go splash your feet there!
10) Yes! It's supposed to bring you luck in love. Fingers crossed!

# PACKING AND PLANNING TIPS

## A Week before Leaving

- Arrange for someone to take care of pets and water plants.

- Email and Print important Documents.

- Get Visa and vaccines if needed.

- Check for travel warnings.

- Stop mail and newspaper.

- Notify Credit Card companies where you are going.

- Passports and photo identification is up to date.

- Pay bills.

- Copy important items and download travel Apps.

- Start collecting small bills for tips.

- Have post office hold mail while you are away.

- Check weather for the week.

- Car inspected, oil is changed, and tires have the correct pressure.

- Check airline luggage restrictions.

- Download Apps needed for your trip.

# Right Before Leaving

- Contact bank and credit cards to tell them your location.

- Clean out refrigerator.

- Empty garbage cans.

- Lock windows.

- Make sure you have the proper identification with you.

- Bring cash for tips.

- Remember travel documents.

- Lock door behind you.

- Remember wallet.

- Unplug items in house and pack chargers.

- Change your thermostat settings.

- Charge electronics, and prepare camera memory cards.

# READ OTHER
# GREATER THAN A TOURIST
# BOOKS

*Greater Than a Tourist- California: 50 Travel Tips from Locals*

*Greater Than a Tourist- Salem Massachusetts USA 50 Travel Tips from a Local by Danielle Lasher*

*Greater Than a Tourist United States: 50 Travel Tips from Locals*

*Greater Than a Tourist- St. Croix US Birgin Islands USA: 50 Travel Tips from a Local by Tracy Birdsall*

*Greater Than a Tourist- Montana: 50 Travel Tips from a Local by Laurie White*

*Children's Book: Charlie the Cavalier Travels the World by Lisa Rusczyk Ed. D.*

# > TOURIST

Follow us on Instagram for beautiful travel images:
http://Instagram.com/GreaterThanATourist

Follow *Greater Than a Tourist* on Amazon.

CZYKPublishing.com

# > TOURIST

At *Greater Than a Tourist*, we love to share travel tips with you. How did we do? What guidance do you have for how we can give you better advice for your next trip? Please send your feedback to GreaterThanaTourist@gmail.com as we continue to improve the series. We appreciate your constructive feedback. Thank you.

# METRIC CONVERSIONS

## TEMPERATURE

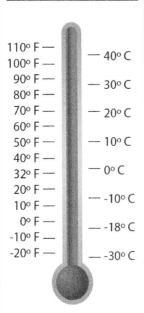

110° F —
100° F —
90° F —
80° F —
70° F —
60° F —
50° F —
40° F —
32° F —
20° F —
10° F —
0° F —
-10° F —
-20° F —

— 40° C
— 30° C
— 20° C
— 10° C
— 0° C
— -10° C
— -18° C
— -30° C

### To convert F to C:

Subtract 32, and then multiply by 5/9 or .5555.

### To Convert C to F:

Multiply by 1.8 and then add 32.

### 32F = 0C

## LIQUID VOLUME

To Convert:................Multiply by
U.S. Gallons to Liters................ 3.8
U.S. Liters to Gallons ...............26
Imperial Gallons to U.S. Gallons 1.2
Imperial Gallons to Liters....... 4.55
Liters to Imperial Gallons ........22
**1 Liter = .26 U.S. Gallon**
**1 U.S. Gallon = 3.8 Liters**

## DISTANCE

**To convert .............Multiply by**
Inches to Centimeters ....2.54
Centimeters to Inches ........39
Feet to Meters...................... .3
Meters to Feet .................3.28
Yards to Meters ..................91
Meters to Yards ...............1.09
Miles to Kilometers .........1.61
Kilometers to Miles............ .62
**1 Mile = 1.6 km**
**1 km = .62 Miles**

## WEIGHT

1 Ounce  =  .28 Grams
1 Pound  =  .4555 Kilograms
1 Gram  =  .04 Ounce
1 Kilogram  =  2.2 Pounds

83

# TRAVEL QUESTIONS

- Do you bring presents home to family or friends after a vacation?

- Do you get motion sick?

- Do you have a favorite billboard?

- Do you know what to do if there is a flat tire?

- Do you like a sun roof open?

- Do you like to eat in the car?

- Do you like to wear sun glasses in the car?

- Do you like toppings on your ice cream?

- Do you use public bathrooms?

- Did you bring a cell phone and does it have power?

- Do you have a form of identification with you?

- Have you ever been pulled over by a cop?

- Have you ever given money to a stranger on a road trip?

- Have you ever taken a road trip with animals?

- Have you ever gone on a vacation alone?

- Have you ever run out of gas?

- If you could move to any place in the world, where would it be?

- If you could travel anywhere in the world, where would you travel?

- If you could travel in any vehicle, which one would it be?

- If you had three things to wish for from a magic genie, what would they be?

- If you have a driver's license, how many times did it take you to pass the test?

- What are you the most afraid of on vacation?

- What do you want to get away from the most when you are on vacation?

- What foods smell bad to you?

- What item do you bring on ever trip with you away from home?

- What makes you sleepy?

- What song would you love to hear on the radio when you're cruising on the highway?

- What travel job would you want the least?

- What will you miss most while you are away from home?

- What is something you always wanted to try?

- What is the best road side attraction that you ever saw?

- What is the farthest distance you ever biked?

- What is the farthest distance you ever walked?

- What is the weirdest thing you needed to buy while on vacation?

- What is your favorite candy?

- What is your favorite color car?

- What is your favorite family vacation?

- What is your favorite food?

- What is your favorite gas station drink or food?

- What is your favorite license plate design?

- What is your favorite restaurant?

- What is your favorite smell?

- What is your favorite song?

- What is your favorite sound that nature makes?

- What is your favorite thing to bring home from a vacation?

- What is your favorite vacation with friends?

- What is your favorite way to relax?

- Where is the farthest place you ever traveled in a car?

- Where is the farthest place you ever went North, South, East and West?

- Where is your favorite place in the world?

- Who is your favorite singer?

- Who taught you how to drive?

- Who will you miss the most while you are away?

- Who if the first person you will contact when you get to your destination?

- Who brought you on your first vacation?

- Who likes to travel the most in your life?

- Would you rather be hot or cold?

- Would you rather drive above, below, or at the speed limited?

- Would you rather drive on a highway or a back road?

- Would you rather go on a train or a boat?

- Would you rather go to the beach or the woods?

## TRAVEL BUCKET LIST

1.

2.

3.

4.

5.

6.

7.

8.

9.

10.

NOTES

Printed in Great Britain
by Amazon

17261190R00061